THE WORLD'S BEST SIMPLE

BAR TRICKS

Ryan—

To My
showman
with love!
Jen

THE WORLD'S BEST SIMPLE

BAR TRICKS

DOUG LANSKY

ILLUSTRATED BY MELISSA RANDS

A DELL TRADE PAPERBACK

A DELL TRADE PAPERBACK
Published by
Dell Publishing
a division of
Bantam Doubleday Dell Publishing Group, Inc.
1540 Broadway
New York, New York 10036

Library of Congress Cataloging in Publication Data
Lansky, Doug.
The world's best simple bar tricks / Doug Lansky.
          p.   cm.
ISBN 0-440-50826-6
1. Magic tricks.   2. Drinking games.   I. Title.
GV1559.L35   1998
793.8—dc21   98-18132
CIP

Printed in the United States of America

Published simultaneously in Canada

November 1998

10   9   8   7   6   5   4

FFG

To the travelers and bartenders
around the world who shared their
tricks with me.

Contents

Contents

Contents

Introduction

I've traveled all over the world as a journalist, and on my journeys I have found that wherever there are bars, there are bar tricks. From Nepal to Norway, Turkey to Thailand, Greece to Guatemala—every bartender seems to have a trick or two. I began collecting these tricks in my journal, trading with people for new tricks along the way. After six years and more than sixty countries, I had quite a collection.

Unlike magic tricks, bar tricks require virtually no skill. The props for these tricks can be found easily in bars, restaurants, and even your own home. So sit back, have fun, and enjoy!

1. The Walking Coin (SPAIN)

Santiago de Compostela, Spain, has a bar named "Paris" and another named "Dakar." There are about twenty bars located between them. Naturally, students in this town have developed their own Paris to Dakar rally—endurance bar hopping. It was somewhere along this route that I learned this trick.

🍸 **What You Need:** a glass, two quarters, and one dime

🍸 **The Trick:** Get the dime out from under the glass while staying six inches away from the glass in all directions.

The Setup

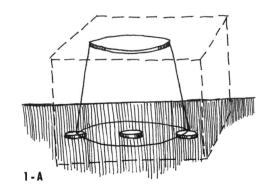

DIAGRAM 1-A Using a table with a fabric tablecloth, place the glass on the quarters and the dime between the quarters, under the glass.

1 - A

 How It Works

DIAGRAM 1-B Use your index fingernail to scratch the tablecloth along the threads that the dime is resting on. The coin will slowly appear to "walk" out from under the glass.

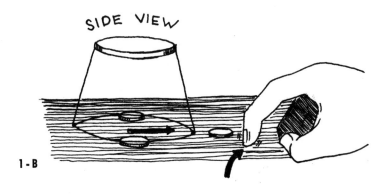

SIDE VIEW

1 - B

2. The Cork Escape (COLORADO)

At a restaurant in Colorado, a waiter put a bottle with a cork in it on the table. "Try to get it out," he challenged us. My family just stared at it. My dad tried sucking it out. My mom tried jabbing it with her knife.

"Easy," I said, taking the bottle and raising it over my head.

"No breaking the bottle," the waiter told me. "At least not on my shift."

What You Need: a wine bottle, a cork, and a cloth napkin

The Trick: Get the cork out without breaking the bottle.

The Cork Escape

 The Setup

DIAGRAM 2-A Push a cork into an empty
wine bottle.

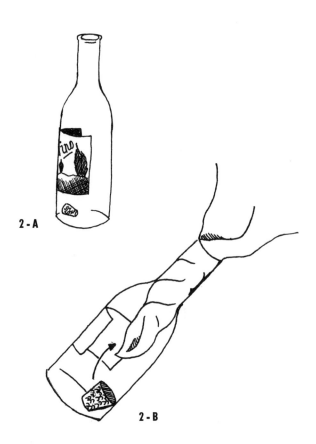

2 - A

 How It Works

DIAGRAM 2-B Twist the cloth napkin
into the bottle.

2 - B

DIAGRAM 2-C Jiggle the bottle until the cork falls lengthwise into the napkin fold.

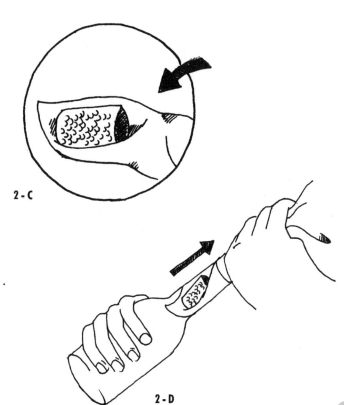

2-C

DIAGRAM 2-D Pull on the napkin . . .

2-D

DIAGRAM 2-E and the cork pops out.

Tip: This trick works better with a lightly starched napkin.

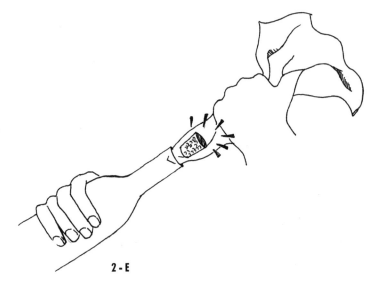

2-E

3. Pushing a Dollar Through a Lemon (ITALY)

I first saw this trick in Bologna using Italian lira and a tomato. The Dutch traveler who performed it in the hotel lobby assured me his own currency, the guilder, was strong enough to pass through a lemon. If you do it carefully, a dollar is strong enough, too.

What You Need: a lemon and a dollar bill

The Trick: Pass the dollar through the lemon.

How It Works

DIAGRAM 3-A Fold one corner of the bill down.

3-A

DIAGRAM 3-B Roll the bill tightly, keeping the point sharp.

3-B

DIAGRAM 3-C Insert the point into the lemon and keep twisting and pushing until the bill passes through.

Tip: This trick works best with a very ripe lemon.

3-C

4. The World's Heaviest Matchbox
(SOUTH AFRICA)

There's just one youth hostel in the ostrich-racing town of Oudtshoorn. After an embarrassing attempt at ostrich riding—I managed to stay on for about twenty seconds—at one of the nearby farms, I returned to the hostel to find a group of Norwegians gathered around a table attempting this trick. When I stuck my head in to take a look, I couldn't see what was so difficult about lifting a matchbox with two fingers . . . until they invited me to try. This trick made the ostrich riding seem easy.

 What You Need: a cigarette package and a box of matches

☿ The Trick

DIAGRAM 4-A Lift the box of matches onto the cigarette package with your index and ring fingers while keeping your middle finger firmly on the table.

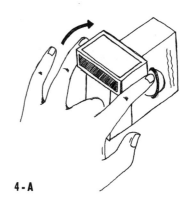

4-A

☿ The Setup

DIAGRAM 4-B Place the cigarette package on its edge and set the matchbox at one end of the package.

4-B

How It Works

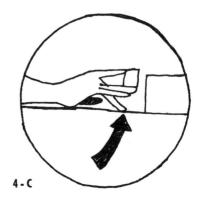

DIAGRAM 4-C Push down hard on your middle finger.

4 - C

DIAGRAM 4-D Lift the matchbox an inch, pull your hand back slightly, and straighten your middle finger.

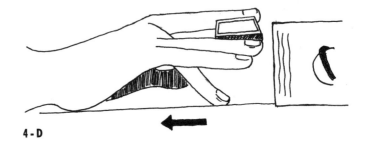

4 - D

DIAGRAM 4-E Push forward and up,
lifting the matchbox.

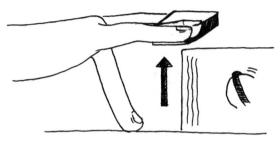

4-E

5. The Match Split (BELGIUM)

This trick is contributed by this book's illustrator, Melissa, who got it from her Belgian boyfriend, Bas, and passed it on to me in France by phone from London. Due to the length of time it took her to explain it—she reversed the charges—I can safely say that this is the most expensive trick in the book.

What You Need: a match

The Trick

DIAGRAM 5-A Split the match in half—lengthwise.

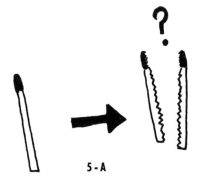

5-A

 **How It Works**

DIAGRAM 5-B Light the match and let it burn completely.

5-B

DIAGRAM 5-C Lick your palms and place the burnt match on the bottom of one palm.

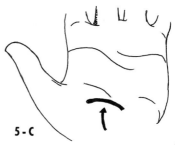

5-C

The Match Split

DIAGRAM 5-D Press your palms together firmly for several seconds.

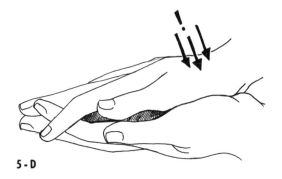

5-D

DIAGRAM 5-E Separate your hands gently and there will be half a match on each hand.

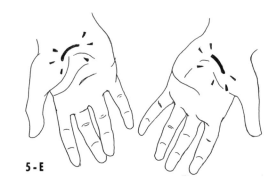

5-E

6. Stick the Bottle (COLORADO)

As I recall, a disproportionate amount of the college years are spent at parties, fighting your way to the keg. (The time left over is divided between searching your room for overdue library books, sleeping in, skiing, and in a few rare cases, attending classes.) At one party, someone must have brought his own bottle, probably so he could demonstrate this trick. It's the one thing I remember learning while inside a fraternity house.

 What You Need: a beer bottle

 The Trick: Pick up the bottle.

Stick the Bottle

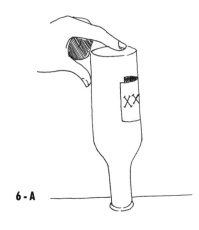

6 - A

 The Setup

DIAGRAM 6-A   Place an empty beer bottle upside down on a table. Put your index finger on top and your thumb on the side of the bottle.

 How It Works

DIAGRAM 6-B   Wipe all moisture off the bottle and dry your thumb and index fingers completely.

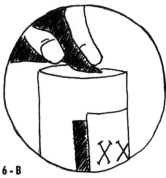

6 - B

DIAGRAM 6-C Put your index finger and thumb on the bottle immediately after drying . . . and lift.

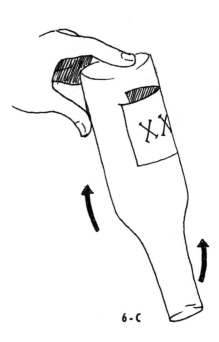

6-C

7. The Disappearing Cigarette (SWEDEN)

At a bar in the university town of Lund, Sweden, the guy next to me offered me a cigarette. When I said, "No thanks," he casually made the cigarette disappear and went back to his drink. It cost me a shot of aquavit to learn this sleight of hand.

 What You Need: a cigarette

 The Trick: Make the cigarette disappear.

How It Works

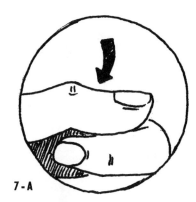

DIAGRAM 7-A   Lick your thumb above the knuckle.

7-A

DIAGRAM 7-B   Discreetly push the non-filter end of the cigarette against your wet thumb with your index finger.

7-B

The Disappearing Cigarette

DIAGRAM 7-C Quickly open your hand.

7-C

DIAGRAM 7-D The cigarette becomes hidden behind the thumb . . .

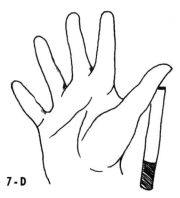

7-D

DIAGRAM 7-E and disappears.

7-E

8. The Unbreaking Match (NEW ZEALAND)

There's plenty of adrenaline in Queenstown, the bungee-jumping, jet-boating capital of the Southern Hemisphere. A local Kiwi taught me this piece of "magic" over a chocolate-banana pizza, which is tastier than it sounds.

 What You Need: a bar towel and two matches

 The Trick: "Unbreak" a match.

The Setup

DIAGRAM 8-A Secretly insert one match into the bar towel's seam.

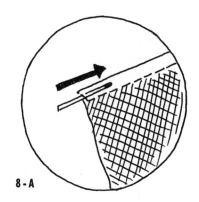

8-A

DIAGRAM 8-B Hold a match in your hand.

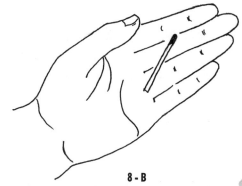

8-B

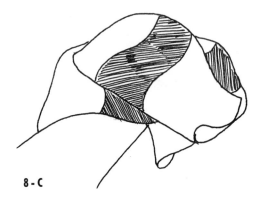

DIAGRAM 8-C Place your hand with the match under the bar towel.

8-C

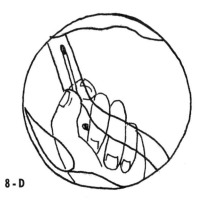

DIAGRAM 8-D While holding the match with your middle and ring fingers, grab the corner of the bar towel with the hidden match with your thumb and index finger.

8-D

DIAGRAM 8-E   With the towel still covering your hand, let someone break the match hidden in the seam.

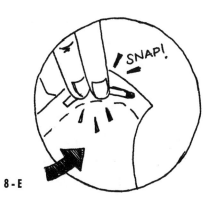

8-E

DIAGRAM 8-F   Let the unbroken match fall out of your hand as you shake the bar towel. The broken match will remain in the towel's seam.

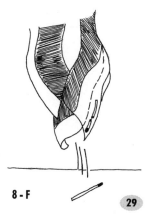

8-F

9. The Magnetic Cigarette (COLOMBIA)

Santa Marta, on Colombia's northern coast, is the popular departure town for treks to the Lost City, a fourteenth-century village abandoned by the Tayrona Indians that had been hidden by thick jungle until 1984. Nowadays, it's about as lost as Cleveland. I stayed in Santa Marta only long enough to pick up some trekking supplies and learn this trick from a chain-smoking Austrian mountain guide.

 What You Need: a cigarette

 The Trick: Make the cigarette appear to move on its own.

How It Works

DIAGRAM 9-A Lay the cigarette on a table and circle your finger around it, pretending to magnetize it.

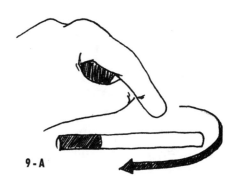

9 - A

DIAGRAM 9-B Subtly blow the cigarette while you pretend to push it forward with your magnetized finger.

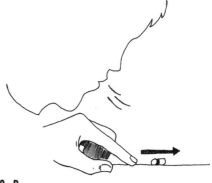

9 - B

DIAGRAM 9-C The cigarette will appear to roll on its own.

Tip: This trick works best on a smooth, even table. It also helps if music is playing so your audience won't hear you blowing.

9 - C

10. The Matchstick Maneuver (EGYPT)

Things move so slowly in the traveler hangout town of Dahab, where drinking a mango shake is considered an aerobic activity, it's amazing somebody managed to work up enough energy to show me this match trick. Fortunately, it only requires moving two hands.

 What You Need: two matches

 The Trick

DIAGRAM 10-A Separate the matches so they appear to pass through each other.

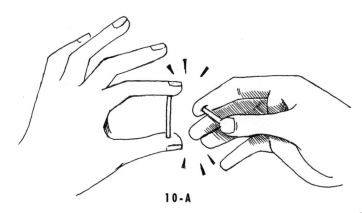

10-A

The Matchstick Maneuver

 ## The Setup

DIAGRAM 10-B Place the matches between the index fingers and thumbs of both hands so the matches are interlocked. The left hand's match should be below the right hand's match.

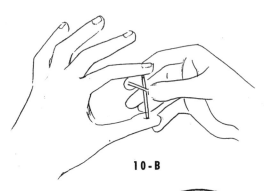

10-B

 ## How It Works

DIAGRAM 10-C Push one end of the match into the pad of the left index finger for ten to twenty seconds.

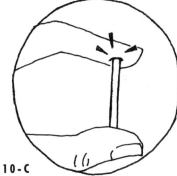

10-C

DIAGRAM 10-D Pull the match in the left hand a few millimeters away from the thumb and let the match in the right hand pass through.

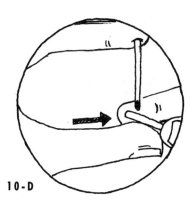

10-D

DIAGRAM 10-E Quickly close the gap.

Tip: The faster you can do this, the more realistic it looks.

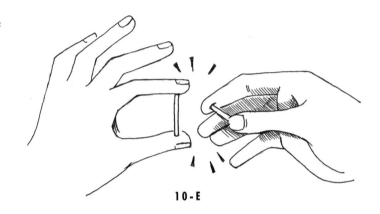

10-E

11. The Rubber Band Pass (LAS VEGAS)

David Copperfield was sold out. I couldn't afford to see Seigfried and Roy. So, between a few rounds at the quarter slots, I walked by a magic shop, where I saw this trick being performed.

 What You Need: two rubber bands

 The Trick

DIAGRAM 11-A Make the rubber bands appear to separate.

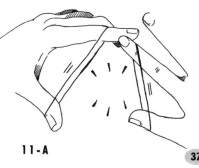

11-A

The Rubber Band Pass

 ## The Setup

DIAGRAM 11-B Stretch the rubber bands across the thumbs and index fingers of both hands so the bands are interlocked.

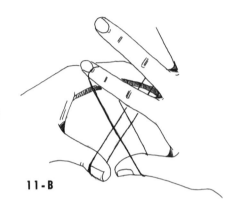

11-B

 ## How It Works

DIAGRAM 11-C As if to simply show the rubber bands are interlocked, stretch them against each other. But pinch the rubber band on the right hand between the index and middle fingers.

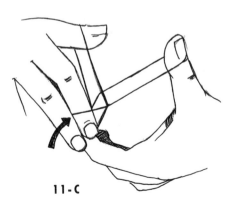

11-C

DIAGRAM 11-D Rotate the right hand slightly so the rubber band rolls onto the middle finger.

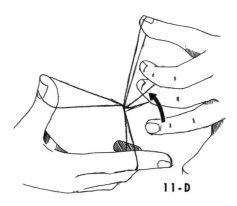

11-D

DIAGRAM 11-E This frees up the index finger to enter the loop near the thumb.

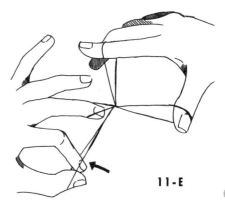

11-E

The Rubber Band Pass

DIAGRAM 11-F   Spread the rubber band with the index finger as the middle finger is removed from the loop.

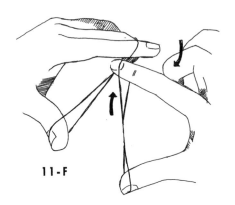

11-F

DIAGRAM 11-G   And bring the rubber bands back together.

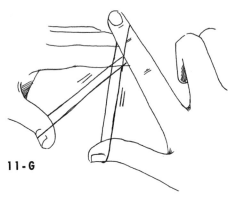

11-G

DIAGRAM 11-H Then "magically" pull them apart.

Tip: This trick should be done in a single fluid motion while you appear to be simply stretching the rubber bands against each other. It may take some practice to get it right.

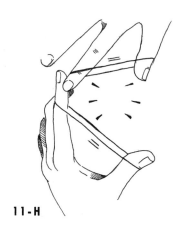

11-H

12. The Coin Pick (AUSTRALIA)

Pat and John, two Irishmen on my four-wheeling safari on Fraser Island, the world's largest sand island, entertained us around the campfire each night with their vast repertoire of dirty jokes. When they finally ran out of jokes on the last evening, they offered this trick.

What You Need: a hat and five different coins

The Trick: Pick the selected coin out of the hat.

The Setup: Place the coins in the hat and let someone secretly pick a coin, then put it back in the hat.

How It Works: Tell the person who selects the coin to hold it to her forehead and concentrate on the coin for ten seconds. When you reach into the hat with your eyes closed, just feel for the warmest coin. The body heat gives it away.

13. The Hanging Ash (ENGLAND)

As a nonsmoker, smoking had never impressed me. That was until I walked into a pub in Covent Garden and saw a woman casually smoking the longest stick of ash I ever saw. With some begging and a pint of Guinness, I eventually learned how it worked.

 What You Need: a cigarette and a pin

 The Trick

DIAGRAM 13-A   Make the cigarette ash cling to the cigarette.

13-A

How It Works

DIAGRAM 13-B Secretly insert a pin before smoking.

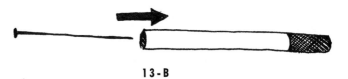

13-B

14. The Four Coin Move (FRANCE)

It seemed impossible. I asked my friend, a graphic designer in Paris, to explain the rules again. Then I just sat there and stared at the coins, hoping my will alone would move them into alignment.

What You Need: four quarters

The Trick

DIAGRAM 14-A Move the quarters to form a straight line while observing the rules.

14-A

The Four Coin Move

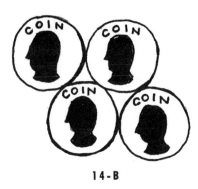

14-B

 The Setup

DIAGRAM 14-B   Place the four quarters together in this formation.

 The Rules

1. Move only one coin at a time.
2. When the coin being moved stops, it must be touching at least two other coins.
3. Coins cannot be placed on top of each other.
4. A coin cannot be used to push another coin.

How It Works

DIAGRAM 14-C

Step 1

Step 3

Step 2

Step 4

The Four Coin Move

DIAGRAM 14-D

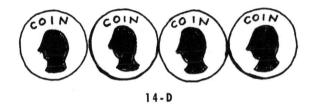

14-D

15. Counting Matches (BOTSWANA)

After my safari group walked in the Okavango Delta, Botswana—where, combined, the only weapon we had to defend ourselves against elephants, lions, and leopards was my Swiss army knife—we played this game to unwind at our campsite. After playing for twenty minutes with an Aussie who had a matching Oktoberfest shirt and baseball hat, it occurred to me that I had not won a game yet. Eventually, I figured out why.

 What You Need: fifteen matches

The Trick: Find a partner and take turns removing either one, two, or three matches per turn. Don't get stuck with the last match.

Counting Matches

 The Setup: Line up the matches on the floor or table.

 How It Works: To leave her with the last match, you need to leave her with five matches. To get to five, you need to leave her with nine matches. To get to nine, you need to leave her with thirteen. Which means, if you go first, take two.

Once you're on track, an easier way of thinking is to total four. If she takes one, you take three. If she takes two, you take two. And if she takes one, you take three.

16. The Triangle Construction (INDIA)

In the city of Udaipur in northwest India, the James Bond film, *Octopussy*, which was filmed there, plays every evening in one of the local restaurants. After the film, travelers passing through town swap stories and drink cheap beer. From another table, I watched a young Israeli backpacker demonstrate this three-dimensional trick.

What You Need: Six matches

The Trick: Make four equilateral triangles out of six matches—and no breaking the matches!

How It Works

DIAGRAM 16-A Use three dimensions.

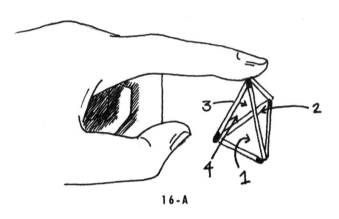

16-A

17. The Headbanger (AUSTRALIA)

When performed properly—as this trick was in a youth hostel bar in Earlie Beach—it will bend a participant's brain unlike most other tricks. It just may be the most entertaining trick in the book. A frustrated and drunken Englishman nearly put his head through the table before the rest of us restrained him.

 What You Need: one coin

 The Trick: Make someone think he has a coin on his forehead.

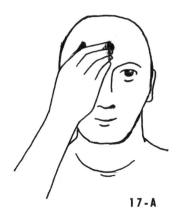

17-A

 How It Works

DIAGRAM 17-A Demonstrate for others. Push the coin to your forehead for several seconds until it stays on its own.

DIAGRAM 17-B Explain that to get the coin to fall off you must gently tap your head on the bar. When you do so, the coin will fall off easily.

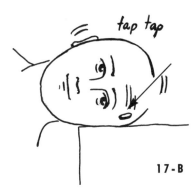

tap tap

17-B

DIAGRAM 17-C Now hold the coin just under your thumbnail and middlefinger nail and push the coin to the forehead of a "friend" for about fifteen seconds.

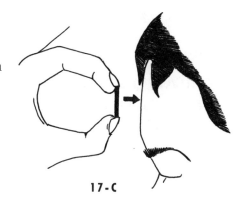

17-C

DIAGRAM 17-D Then pull your hand (and the coin) away quickly, keeping the coin out of view. The person will think the coin is still on his forehead.

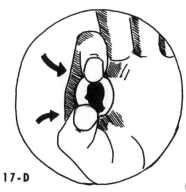

17-D

Note

DIAGRAM 17-E It is good bar trick manners to stop him from whacking his head on the bar before he injures himself.

17-E

18. The Coaster Lift (BRAZIL)

There wasn't much going on in Manaus, Brazil, a city located halfway up the Amazon, while I waited for days in the suffocating heat for my crowded cargo ship to depart. Aside from dodging large spiders in my hotel room, this trick may have been the most useful thing I learned there.

Y **What You Need:** a coaster and a drink

Y **The Trick:** Ask the owner of the drink to lift the upside—down glass off the bar with two fingers without spilling.

The Coaster Lift

♈ The Setup

DIAGRAM 18-A   Place the coaster over a full drink. Flip it over and set it on the bar.

18-A

♈ How It Works

DIAGRAM 18-B   It's a natural vacuum (trust me on this one).

Tip: Make sure the bar isn't wet, or the coaster might stick to the bar.

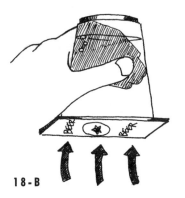

18-B

19. The Submerged Dime Drop (GERMANY)

If you've ever had the urge to go out to your backyard with a case of beer, stand on your deck furniture, and sing stupid drinking songs at the top of your lungs until you fall off and pass out in the shrubs, then I highly recommend a trip to the Oktoberfest in Munich. You can join millions of people from all corners of the world with this same passion. I was in the Haufbrau tent when I saw this trick performed with beer and liter-sized steins.

What You Need: two glasses filled with water, three dimes, and a coaster

The Trick

DIAGRAM 19-A   Invert one full glass on top of the other, then get the three dimes inside.

19-A

The Submerged Dime Drop

 How It Works

DIAGRAM 18-A (FROM PREVIOUS TRICK) Place a coaster over
one glass of water.

18-A

DIAGRAM 19-B Invert the glass with the coaster and set it on the
second glass of water.

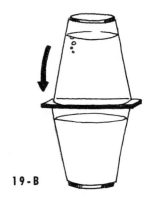

19-B

DIAGRAM 19-C Steady both glasses with one hand while you yank the coaster out with the other. You will lose a few drops of water while doing this, but not much if you're quick.

19-C

DIAGRAM 19-D Move the top glass about a millimeter to the left while holding both glasses with the left hand. Use the right hand to quickly push a dime between the lips of the glasses. Repeat with remaining dimes.

Tip: I recommend that you practice this trick over the sink using water and cheap glasses.

19-D

20. The Straw Pickup (ARGENTINA)

In Argentina, as in many countries around the world, teachers often don't get the respect and salaries they deserve. Therefore, many are forced to take part-time jobs to augment their income. A physics teacher working a second job in a bar in Buenos Aires opened up my eyes to another use for straws.

What You Need: two plastic straws, one half-straw, and a lighter

The Trick: Pick up the two straws (the bent straw and the half-straw) using a straight third straw.

The Setup

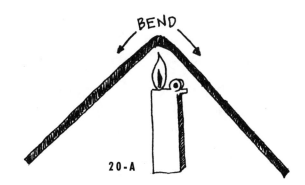

DIAGRAM 20-A   Use a lighter to bend a plastic straw ninety degrees.

DIAGRAM 20-B   Take the half-straw and lean it up against the bent straw to form a tripod.

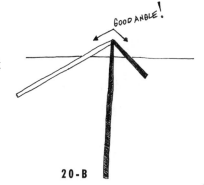

The Straw Pickup

How It Works

DIAGRAM 20-C Put the straight straw under the tripod and push delicately against the bent straw until the half-straw falls to rest on the straw you are holding.

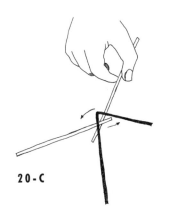

20-C

DIAGRAM 20-D Lift up and the straws will lock together.

Tip: This trick is best performed on a tablecloth or napkin so the straws don't slide.

20-D

21. The Balancing Act (INDONESIA)

As a DJ at Club Med in Bali, holding the headphones to one ear and pushing the mirrored disco ball button got old after a few nights. So I put on a greatest dance hits CD and strolled over to the bar to make use of my monthly allotment of "bar beads" (a unique monetary system using plastic beads in which you spend eight dollars for a Dixie cup full of beer without realizing it). The bartender had enough time to show me this trick before I had to change the CD.

What You Need: a glass, a fork, a spoon, a toothpick, and some matches

The Trick

DIAGRAM 21-A Balance the spoon and fork on the edge of the glass with the shortest possible toothpick.

21-A

How It Works

DIAGRAM 21-B Push the spoon in between the prongs of the fork so they lock together.

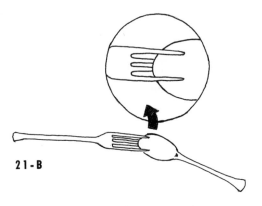

21-B

DIAGRAM 21-C Put the toothpick through the top prong of the fork.

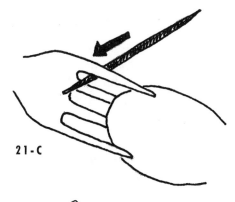

21-C

DIAGRAM 21-D Balance the toothpick on the edge of the glass and light the ends of the toothpick. The ends will burn out naturally when they reach the glass edge and fork.

21-D

22. The Levitating Olive (GREECE)

It is hard to get far from an olive anywhere in this country, but it wasn't until I landed on the island of Rhodes that I learned another use for this marinated treat.

What You Need: a brandy glass, an olive, and an ashtray

The Trick: Without touching the olive, get it into the ashtray while keeping the glass upside down and without moving the ashtray.

The Setup

DIAGRAM 22-A Place the brandy glass over the olive, one foot away from the ashtray.

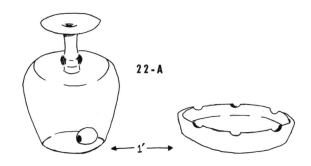

22-A

1'

 How It Works

DIAGRAM 22-B Spin the glass and the olive will climb up into the widest part. While continuing to spin, lift the glass.

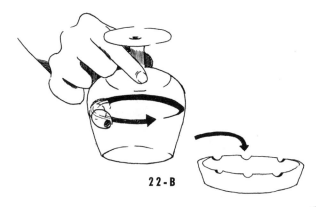

22-B

DIAGRAM 22-C Stop spinning once the glass is directly over the ashtray and let the olive drop.

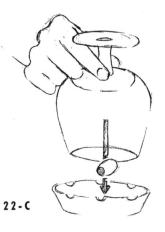

22-C

23. The Vacuum Pump (INDONESIA)

Shadow puppet shows, the most famous tourist spectacle of Jakarta, weren't getting my adrenaline pumping. I left after thirty minutes and made for a bar where a German traveler showed me this little physics experiment.

Y **What You Need:** a glass, two matches, two slices of lime, and an ashtray half filled with water.

Y **The Trick:** Move the water from the ashtray into the glass without pouring the water from one into the other.

How It Works

DIAGRAM 23-A Float the limes in the water and stick the matches into them. Then light the matches and cover them with the glass. The glass should fit inside the ashtray.

23-A

DIAGRAM 23-B As the matches burn off the oxygen, the water runs up into the glass.

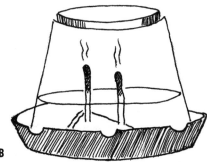

23-B

24. The Shotglass Spill (FIJI)

Not only did Jeremaia give me a free ride to the firewalking demonstration, he also insisted on buying me a drink to welcome me to his country. Over a rum and cola I got a taste of Fijian hospitality while getting a lesson in surface tension.

What You Need: a shotglass filled with water to the top and a stack of dimes

The Trick: Drop ten dimes in the shotglass without spilling any water.

How It Works

DIAGRAM 24-A Gently place a dime on the edge of the shotglass and let it slide down the side to the bottom. Repeat with nine other dimes.

24-A

DIAGRAM 24-B Surface tension will keep it from spilling.

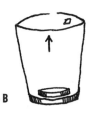

24-B

25. The Dollar Roll Out
(ST. JOHN'S, UNITED STATES VIRGIN ISLANDS)

Depending on where you shop in the Caribbean, you can actually find a bottle of rum cheaper than a bottle of Coca-Cola. While I was working on a yacht in the Virgin Islands in an unsuccessful attempt to hitchhike by sea from Florida to Venezuela, I picked up this trick. Because of the balance required, the captain could perform it only while we were anchored in a calm bay.

Y **What You Need:** a dollar bill and an empty beer bottle

Y **The Trick:** Get the bill out without touching or knocking over the bottle.

The Dollar Roll Out

 The Setup

DIAGRAM 25-A Place a beer bottle upside down on top of a bill.

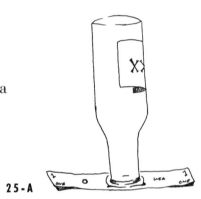

25-A

 How It Works

DIAGRAM 25-B Roll the bill toward the bottle.

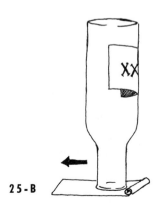

25-B

DIAGRAM 25-C When the rolled bill touches the bottle, use it to gently push the bottle.

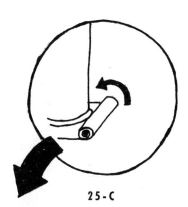

25 - C

DIAGRAM 25-D Keep pushing until you pull the bill free.

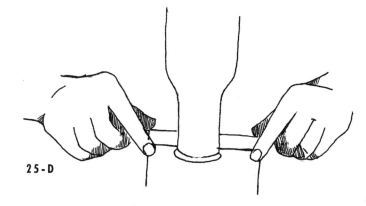

25 - D

26. Smoke Swallow (JORDAN)

A Swiss traveler at a hummus (a spread made of chickpeas) cafe in Amman had me convinced he was actually swallowing the cigarette smoke. This is perhaps the only trick that involves smoking that can be done easily by nonsmokers.

Y **What You Need:** a lit cigarette

Y **The Trick:** Take a deep drag from a lit cigarette and "swallow the smoke" so that when you exhale, no smoke comes out.

How It Works

DIAGRAM 26-A You don't actually inhale. You slowly blow out. This makes the end of the cigarette glow as if you were inhaling.

Tip: This trick requires a little acting.

26-A

27. The Bending Cigarette

One of the popular hangouts in postwar Sarajevo is the Internet Cafe. It's worth noting, however, that there's no Internet access. In fact, there's not a single computer. But it does have fluorescent-painted land mines attached to the ceiling! I picked up this trick from an aid worker there.

What You Need: a cigarette and a lighter

The Trick

DIAGRAM 27-A Holding a cigarette in both hands, bend it without breaking it.

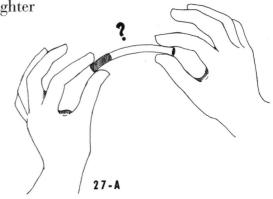

27-A

How It Works: Light the cigarette and take about three long drags. The cigarette will bend (watch your fingers on the lit end!).

28. The Bouncing Match (NAMIBIA)

After two days on safari in Etosha National Park trying to spot lions in the tall yellow grass and leopards in the bushes, I thought my eyesight was pretty good. But in one of the rest camps my vision was not keen enough to see how an Englishman (wearing a safari outfit, no less) made a match bounce around on its own.

What You Need: two matches

The Trick: Make the second (resting) match appear to jump on its own.

The Bouncing Match

28-A

 The Setup

DIAGRAM 28-A Hold one match between your index finger and thumb and resting on the nail of your middle finger.

 How It Works

DIAGRAM 28-B Using the index finger, push the first match down hard against the middle finger's nail and slightly forward.

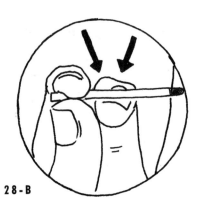

28-B

DIAGRAM 28-C The match will make minute movements along the ridges in the nail, causing the resting match to jump.

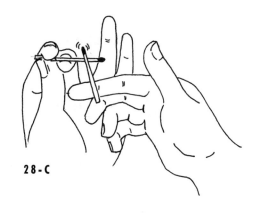

28-C

29. Passing the Coin Through the Hat (ECUADOR)

I didn't expect to find bar tricks in the Otavallo market, where any self-respecting traveler in South America goes to buy a sweater or two. A Danish traveler showed me this trick using his new alpaca hat in the popular Otavallo Pie Shop on the main square.

🍸 **What You Need:** a hat, a glass, and two quarters

🍸 **The Trick**

DIAGRAM 29-A   Make a quarter appear to pass through the hat into the glass.

29-A

The Setup

DIAGRAM 29-B Balance the hat upside down on a glass.

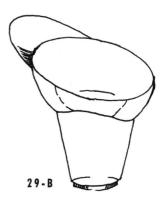

29-B

DIAGRAM 29-C Secretly balance a quarter on the rim of the glass under the hat.

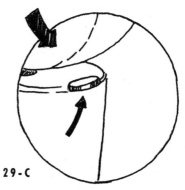

29-C

Passing the Coin Through the Hat

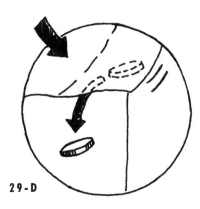

29-D

 How It Works

DIAGRAM 29-D When you throw a quarter into the hat, it will cause the hidden quarter to fall into the glass and make it look as though the quarter passed directly through the hat.

30. The Coaster Pick Trick (NEPAL)

When it's freezing and cloudy, there isn't much to do at the Annapurna Base Camp in Nepal. In our mountain hut, using nine napkins instead of coasters, two Kiwis managed to keep a small, international group of trekkers guessing for an hour with this trick.

🍸 **What You Need:** Nine coasters and a friend who knows the trick

🍸 **The Trick**

 Guess which coaster was selected while your friend points to each coaster and asks, "Is it this one?"

30-A

The Coaster Pick Trick

30-B

The Setup

DIAGRAM 30-B Place the nine coasters on a table in a square formation. While you turn away, have someone in the audience point to a coaster.

How It Works

DIAGRAM 30-C Your friend knows which coaster was selected and she will tell you with the first coaster she points to. How? Each of the nine coasters is like a map.

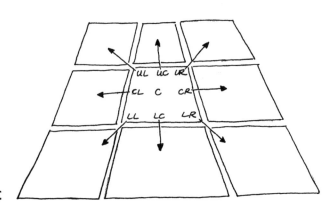

30-C

88

DIAGRAM 30-D The spot on the coaster she points to will indicate which coaster was selected. For example, if she points to the lower left corner of any coaster, that means the lower left coaster was selected. If she points to the center of any coaster, that means it's the middle coaster.

Tip: People will understand that you have some kind of code, but it will likely take them between ten minutes and one hour to figure it out. When people think they know the system, let them try, but encourage them not to blurt out the secret. It then becomes a competition not to be the last to discover it.

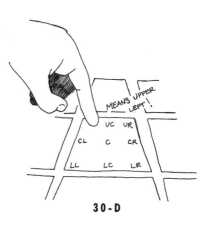

30-D

31. Knuckle Crackers (NEW ZEALAND)

Here's a great way to humble someone twice your size who looks like his level of testosterone is about on par with the national debt figures of a developing nation. Not surprisingly, I learned this trick from a rugby player in New Zealand who had probably broken his own knuckles—out of pride—before learning this trick.

 The Trick

DIAGRAM 31-A To see who can make the loudest sound by whacking his knuckles on the bar . . .

31-A

DIAGRAM 31-B   . . . without breaking any bones.

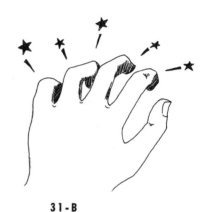

3 1 - B

 ## How It Works

DIAGRAM 31-C   Slap the bar with your fingers at the very last moment, then make a fist again as your hand passes below the bar.

Tip: Works best in a dimly lit bar.

3 1 - C

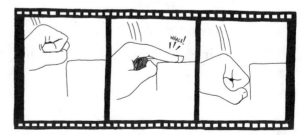

32. No Ash Smoking (MOROCCO)

This trick is as much a play on words as it is a bar trick, so make sure you're showing it to someone with a good sense of humor. While working as a carpet hustler in Marrakech, my friend Ahmed won four dollars off me with this trick.

What You Need: a cigarette and a match or lighter

The Trick

`DIAGRAM 32-A` Ask someone to take three long drags on a lit cigarette without producing any ash.

3 2 - A

How It Works

DIAGRAM 32-B Light the cigarette in the middle.

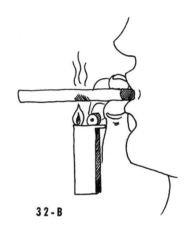

32-B

33. The Chopstick Drop (BOLIVIA)

You wouldn't expect there to be an Israeli club in La Paz, the capital of Bolivia, but with tens of thousands of Israeli travelers passing through every year, El Lobo is actually one of the most popular hangouts in town. I was surprised to see how competitive this simple game became as good friends pitted their reflexes against one another. They were using a pen, but I discovered, in a Bangkok restaurant, that it works a little better with a chopstick.

 What You Need: a chopstick

The Trick

DIAGRAM 33-A When the chopstick is dropped without warning, catch it before it hits the ground.

33-A

 The Setup

DIAGRAM 33-B Hold the chopstick on the ends.

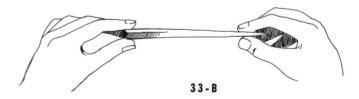

33-B

The Chopstick Drop

DIAGRAM 33-C Ask a volunteer to put one hand six inches above the chopstick, palm down.

33-C

 How It Works

DIAGRAM 33-D Most people try to grab it too quickly. Bend your knees and try to catch it between thigh and shin level.

33-D

34. The Step-Through Business Card (CHILE)

You don't run into many Japanese travelers in South America. So I was surprised when Nori showed up for breakfast at my pension in Puerto Natales on the southern tip of Chilean Patagonia. Business card exchanges are part of the formal greeting in Japan, according to Nori, who announced he would step through his business card after we finished eating.

 What You Need: one business card and a pair of scissors

 The Trick: Step through a business card.

How It Works

DIAGRAM 34-A Fold the card in half.

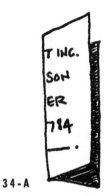

34-A

DIAGRAM 34-B Cut both halves of the card at the same time. Cut as shown by the dotted lines, making the strips as thin as possible.

CUT

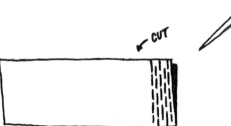

34-B

DIAGRAM 34-C Cut along the fold, but do not cut the last $\frac{1}{16}$ inch on each end.

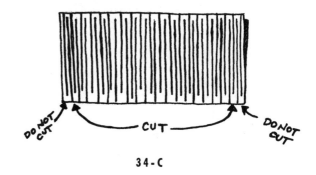

34-C

DIAGRAM 34-D Pull the card open and step through.

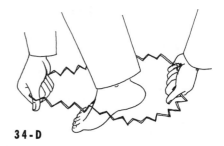

34-D

35. The Liquid Handcuffs (ISRAEL)

I doubt this technique was ever used by the Mossad, but I noticed it was a highly effective restraint for one overeager man in The Underground, a popular pub in Jerusalem. The woman he was trying to hit on just left a full drink on his thumbs and walked out.

What You Need: a glass filled to the top

The Trick: Handcuff someone to the bar with a drink.

How It Works

DIAGRAM 35-A Ask him—for bar trick purposes—to put his thumbs together on the bar.

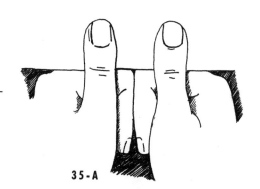

35-A

DIAGRAM 35-B Place a very full drink on his thumbs and say good-bye.

35-B